MERIDIAN

A Raw Thoughts Book

MERIDIAN
A Raw Thoughts Book

John Casey

Other Books in This Series

RAW THOUGHTS: A Mindful Fusion of Poetic and Photographic Art

PHIR PUBLISHING
SAN ANTONIO, TX

Copyright © 2021 by John Casey
Photography © 2021 by Scott Hussey

PHiR Publishing
San Antonio, TX
phirpublishing.com

First Edition: June 2021

All rights reserved. No part of this book may be reproduced without permission. If you would like to use material from the book (other than for review purposes), please contact permissions@phirpublishing.com.

ISBN 978-1-7370627-2-1
LCCN 2021905947

Printed in the United States of America

For Us

meridian | *mə-ˈri-dē-ən* | noun: highest point or stage of development; peak; pathway along which the body's vital energy flows

Thoughts

Foreword	13

I. Affliction

Deference for Despair	16
Enmity	18
Oblivion	20
Someone	22
Teufelskreis	24
Concerning Me	26
Red Pill Blue Pill	28
Terminal	30
My Lethean Reprisal	32
Broken	34

II. Existence

Love Letter from a Narcissist — 38
Duplicity — 40
Easy Prey — 42
Halfway to Nowhere — 44
Sanctimony — 46
Anyone — 48
Dominion — 50
Indemnity — 52
Scruple — 54
Lenity — 56

III. Reason

Why — 60
Subtleties — 62
That Thing That Was Missing — 64
Keeping in Mind — 66
The Nihility of Everything — 68
Want — 70
Still — 72
Look Inside — 74

IV.   Sight

Clarity 78
Musing 80
Move 82
Spring 84
Au Courant 86
The Lightness of Time 88
Life 90
Keep A Light On 92

V.   Serenity

Reminiscence 96
The Perfect Pair 98
At First Sight 100
Ne Plus Ultra 102
Rhapsody 104
Perfect Day 106
Celestial Reverie 108
This 110
Being Human 112

Φ 115

Acknowledgements 117
About the Author 118

Foreword

"What is reality? An icicle forming in fire." – Dogen Zenji

Consider that what is seen, heard and felt is oftentimes a spurious variation of reality. It is in understanding each unique history of thought that leads up to those sights, those sounds and sentiments, that truth is revealed.

Access to clarity of thought often requires subjugation of emotion. Though they are essential, emotions affect judgement when left unchecked. This can lead to invalid assumptions and flawed perceptions. Facts are misconstrued, correlation is confused with causation and reality begins to depart a path of truth. The goal should be for that reality to be as authentic as possible.

To help us achieve that goal, *Meridian* presents compelling and visceral snapshots of the mind arranged in a way that suggests positive change is possible if certain steps are taken. Each poem within is symbiotically paired with a photograph—a 'raw thought'. By degrees, the book charts a path from the darkest of places to a place of light. If and as they empathize with raw thoughts along that path, the reader can attempt to analyze and understand their thinking as it relates to themselves, to others, and to life in general. Knowledge gained from this awakening frees the mind to interpret the world more accurately.

Meridian addresses analysis and improvement of thought in a manner that is less emotive, more cognitive, and more refined than in this series' first volume, *Raw Thoughts*, and more so than most will instinctively endeavor to understand. This is a distinction that lends itself naturally to a next-level pursuit of clarity and personal growth.

AFFLICTION

Deference for Despair

Still, sodden, frigid morn.
Muddled shadows.
Scattered, brittle leaves at footfall.
Raven sky, black thoughts, dark path

Listless lost soul in a funereal slate suit
trudging toward the same tired, aimless train.
Preordained purposeless routine,
second verse same as the first

Raw deal, wrong track, wrong song.
Detest it all yet hold it close;
there is esoteric comfort in deference for despair.
When it is all you have, with no way out, love it darkly

Enmity

How could you do such a thing?
Beyond the pale and way too far.
Are you evil? Are you mad?
A malicious, depraved bête noir

What were you thinking today
as you planned this out for me?
It was premeditated,
but karma comes back twice, you see

I loathe your every fiber,
abhor you for your rot and lies
as I rend you limb from limb,
and revel in your cruel demise

Oblivion

It comes on when I am
alone.
In the dark,
usually halfway between
sleep and waking

It is fleeting but I can
sometimes
get it back
for a mindful, masochistic moment.
If I focus

It is not a vision, a sound or smell
or texture, instead
some wretched, untenable amalgam
that cannot, should not,
must be

I need it desperately, to go away…
Terrible and foreboding, it welcomes me
to revel in its sublime, rotted, chaotic perfection.
To dance to the arrhythmic cadence of its deafening silence.
To plummet headlong into its sky and embrace the intangible

Someone

Someone keeps me up at night,
complicating my thoughts.
As sleep arrives,
someone invades my dreams

Someone is in my head,
caressing dark recesses.
Nudging things, catalyzing thoughts
I did not know I had

Someone feels familiar,
hiding in corners and shadows.
I am curious,
but afraid to see a face

I am going mad.
But I think not, this someone is real.
I may have invited them in?
They are not imagined and I am worried

Teufelskreis

Pacing, knowing something is wrong.
My mind racing aimless, back again, pace.
Turn, turn, turn, I knew all along

Tired of hearing this part of the song,
the record is scratched in such a bad place.
Pacing, knowing something is wrong

Circling year after year, all day long,
losing time in an unwinnable race.
Turn, turn, turn, I knew all along

How do I break free, escape and press on?
Effect real change without fear or disgrace?
Pacing, knowing something is wrong

Cursing the cycle from dusk until dawn
as the beast plots out the steps I retrace,
turn, turn, turn, I knew all along

To make my move soon, I need to be strong,
but will continue for now, just in case.
Pacing, knowing something is wrong.
Turn, turn, turn, I knew all along

Concerning Me

People should not tell me how I feel.
When did anyone start renting space in my head?
Why do they voice their opinions?
Why are they so determined, so invested
in divining my disposition?

I have not let them in; they see and hear
what I want them to see and hear.
My body language may betray me
now and again,
but my mind masquerades

Do they really think their observations,
their deductions are of value, cerebral even?
I am not interested in their innuendo and theories
or their haphazard thought experiments.
I do not relate to them or their invasive, self-serving natures

Are they invested at all
in comprehending themselves?
Do they even know who they are?
I think they should begin there

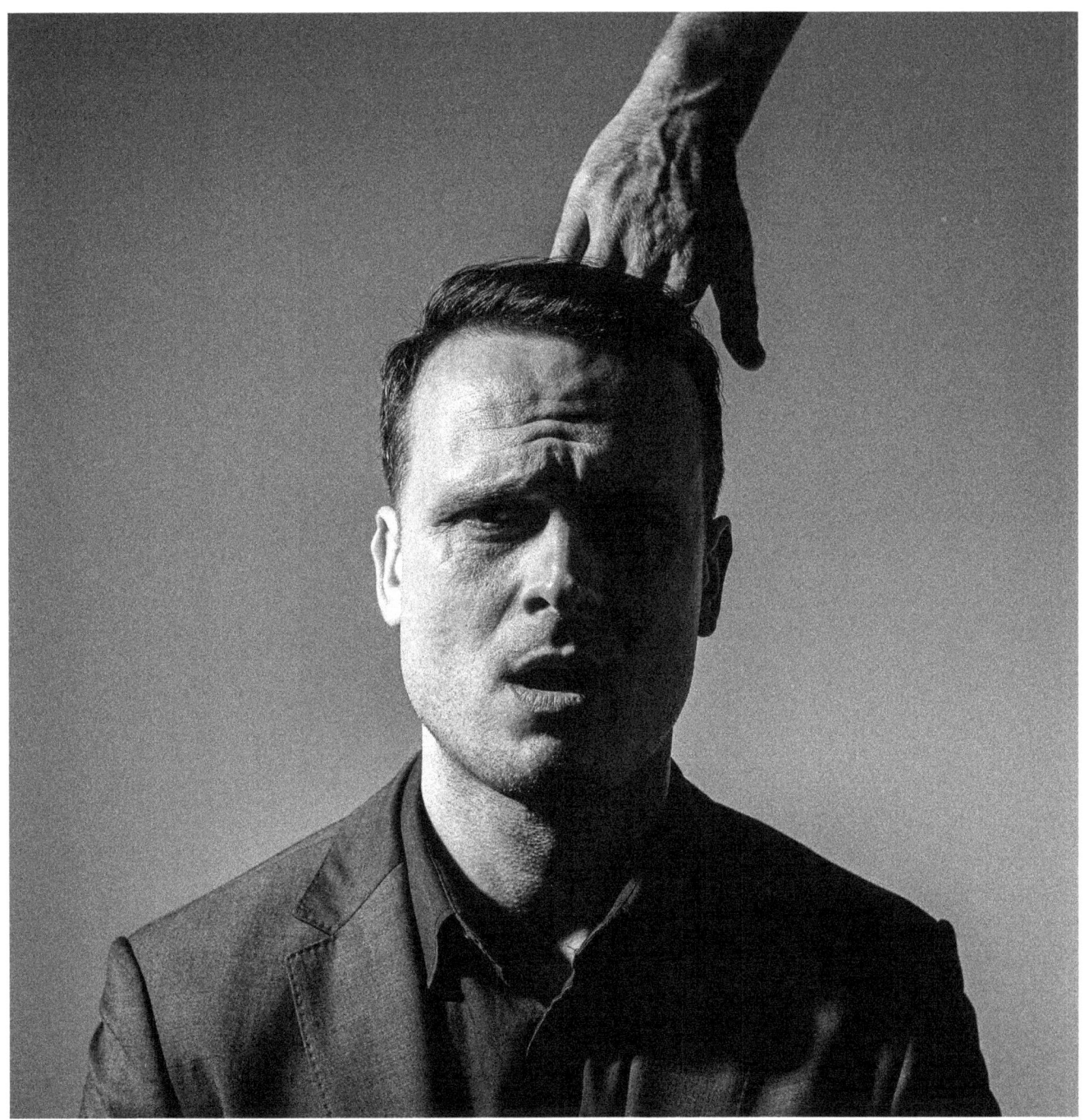

Red Pill Blue Pill

Just got a call from the NSA.
I googled it—sure enough,
the number on my caller ID
was NSA Headquarters.
I almost had a heart attack.
By the time I figured out
it was a hoax
the guy had all my personal information
and bank account numbers

Now I am even more unsettled
than when I was utterly convinced
he was Agent Smith
and I was somehow in some kind of deep trouble

Everything was a little *off,*
and I could not quite figure it out,
and as Smith laid out my dire predicament
I thought about how paranoid I was being and that *Maybe I am in The Matrix.*
I should probably call them—the NSA, *I am just waiting for him to call me 'Mr. Anderson'...*
let them know about this crazy hoax. *I blocked the number. Do you think they already know about the hoax?*
I hope that does not turn out to be a bad move because *They probably do.*
what if the *real* NSA needs to call me? *What if none of this is real?*

Terminal

Two AM, canceled flight.
Tap tapping laptop keys, deadlines and a random playlist.
Cursing the empty concourse, my empty life.
Just me, the guy riding the Zamboni floor cleaner thing, and Falco.
Der Kommissar geht um!
Shifting, cramping in my caustic, black hard-back plastic chair.
Unforgiving, like everything, everyone else

Flagging, anxious to move on, get on.
Move my wallet to my front pocket.
Be smart! You cannot trust anyone these days.
Fatigued, anxious and nauseous now;
that sketchy airport Mexican food
sitting out all day, picked over, decomposing.
I ate it anyway

Sick and tired, uneasy and tapping, the screen is a blur.
No point in trying,
no one to talk to about it and anyway it is
the same thing as yesterday
and the day before and the day before.
Jede Nacht hat ihren Preis!
I just want to fly

My Lethean Reprisal

Their opinions are launched with such animation;
emphatic hand gestures, eyebrows raised, overuse of superlatives.
Too much emphasis on too many flowery adjectives
as they drive their two-ton truck of an ego
headlong through the conversation

Then they change course,
all nuanced and serious,
with thinly veiled assertions
and vague references to remote possibilities
before closing with a speculative grin

But something is not quite right with that smile.
The curve of the lip is good,
however, their eyes are lacking something.
They were lacking all the while.
The eyes do not lie

How can I take them seriously?
What is the goal?
To provoke a response from me, in-kind?
Something that will gift them a little nudge of dopamine?
Are they hoping I will like them?

Perhaps it is more devious.
Arcane,
cabalistic and veiled.
Flamboyantly disguised patronization,
sinister sarcasm, carefully masked

Crafted solely to attain that singular sense of satisfaction
they can receive only after having mentally vanquished someone
with just enough sincerity attached
that I am cornered
into giving them the benefit of the doubt

That is the best, for sure—
to psychologically manipulate someone
in such a way that they are unable to decide
if they have just been commended
or brilliantly deprecated

One thing is for certain,
I will not spend too much time
trying to figure them out.
I will smile, I will nod, I will drink from my glass.
And I will forget them

Broken

Shock no thinking just decide.
Rage from nowhere down inside.
Sensing ruin, cannot tell,
kill the threat or run like hell?

Adrenal-fueled, blinding fear,
cannot see and cannot hear.
Hatred, feelings so intense,
nothing really making sense

All the rot, the black obscene,
twisted places I have been.
The thoughts I had—such a mess.
Lost control, I must confess

Sanity now back in play,
sight returned, at least halfway.
Everything I did was wrong;
wish I knew this all along

Here, take pause, forgive my sin,
I was broken deep within.
My soul hungers for repair,
riven through with loss, lain bare

Existence

Love Letter from a Narcissist

It is not a riddle, crystal clear in black and white.
I do not understand the confusion.
How can you not see it?
You are complicating things where there is no need.
Introducing impertinent facts,
inventing nonexistent extenuating circumstances,
confusing correlation with causation.
No wonder you are so off-track.
And funny, you still think you are right
Pull your head out, wipe away the sand.
Try to focus, because you are all over the place

But wait,
there is some overlap there.
You may be partially correct.
It lacks coherence and yes,
it is neither black nor white in one area.
There is some grey.
What I concluded was crystal clear
appears to have been diffracted a bit.
You may have stumbled onto something.
I recommend you stick with me on this,
my little blind squirrel

Duplicity

Need to be careful.
Just when I think I have it all figured out,
when all is clear,
and I am proud of my hard-won sagacity

Take pause.
Before I write that thought-provoking note,
give that hard-hitting advice,
formulate that grammatically perfect opinion full of gravitas

Reverse-engineer it.
Think about how I got there.
Maybe I forgot the perfect advice I gave yesterday.
It was so significant, right?

If I do not I may find
in all their splendor
my venerable thoughts were founded
on duplicitous grounds

Unless of course, I did not forget.
It was intentional.
In which case,
this is all a waste of time

Easy Prey

You do not answer me, you keep me waiting.
  For what, I cannot fathom.
    As far as I can tell
  you are somewhere between
cannot and will not.
You keep me guessing
 about the why, the where, the when.
    The anticipation mounts

    If I could see you now,
     if I could hear you touch you hold you
if if if...
   But you keep me wondering

 If you cannot, tell me why.
Waiting...
If you will not, tell me why.
 Guessing...
  Tell me where.
    Wondering...
     Tell me when.
       Mounting...

Halfway to Nowhere

Challenged each day to deliver results,
to give and to give up some more.
Measuring sacrifice, every detail.
Continually keeping the score

Steadfastly trying to meet you halfway
while making sure you do the same.
Showing you wherever you are slacking
and steering clear of any blame

Do not point toward me, point at yourself,
I finished my fifty percent.
After recounting each good deed I did
you will have to concede, repent

Then low and behold, unhappy again.
Everything I gave, not enough.
As a result, you stopped short of your half
and now I am calling your bluff

There is no doubt we both tried today but
I am better, I reached the goal.
We will go at it again tomorrow,
my win for today starts the toll

Sanctimony

If God is love, then He must have been near,
though I know He saw fit to endeavor,
when we were still one and you were both here,
to leave with you through a door, forever

Heaven to hell in the blink of an eye.
I have never prayed as hard or as long.
The reason? For now, I cannot descry
why you both left, why our love went so wrong

Come back to me now and prove you are real,
to save me from this and answer my prayer.
All can be right, and right here where I kneel
where I beg this of you on heaven's stair

I never asked for anything before,
my God, with my love, come back through the door

Anyone

Just any love is all I could want,
everything I ever need.
There are those who think they know better
but no one knows, except me

I can envision just any kiss,
meant just for my lips, so sweet.
At random, from someone without whom
my life is so incomplete

Happenchance sparks with no matter who,
waiting for love to arrive.
To anyone, here I am, longing,
as long as I am alive

Dominion

Cautiously serious, tiptoeing a line between feigned compassion and accusation. They say, *"You are almost right, in an uncertain, narrow scope of the thing. We understand where you are coming from, but it is a circular logic of sorts. And it does not reconcile with the facts, as they are."* In their grey suits, with their grey hair. And then they say, *"The bottom line is, accountability lies with you."* At least there is some reference to the lies, though it helps nothing. Thinly veiled is the language of the powerful.

And they sit, elbows propped on their heavy, ornately carved mahogany desk stacked with dusty, dogma-laden volumes. Heads bent forward enough to focus just over the top of their dull gold, wire-rimmed reading glasses. As if that is the reason they are looking down on you. Hand at the ready near a black antique fountain pen set neatly aside the sheet of paper that somehow, with a stroke, makes everything so cautiously explained, however so thinly veiled, however so nauseatingly wrong, right.

Indemnity

Unrelenting rue within,
a toxic, chill despair.
Guilt, regret, a covered sin,
I have to fight for air

Needing it to melt away,
if prayer could make it so...
Sublimation, day by day,
attempt to let it go

Months go by, unfold to years,
the venom courses strong.
Prayers unanswered, lurking fears,
and life travails along

Scruple

With head down and eyes tightly closed,
the riddle unsolved in my mind.
A vision of bliss now exposed
as my life begins to unwind

Safety, regret, or love with pain,
a choice fraught with complexity.
Sense of balance begins to wane,
threat of loss mocks my sanity

A fool chooses nothing or all
and ends up completely alone.
The safe path is a coward's pall
only a weak man could condone

I raise my head, eyes open wide,
and realize my heart is now set.
Love will abide the pain inside
and nothing is left to regret

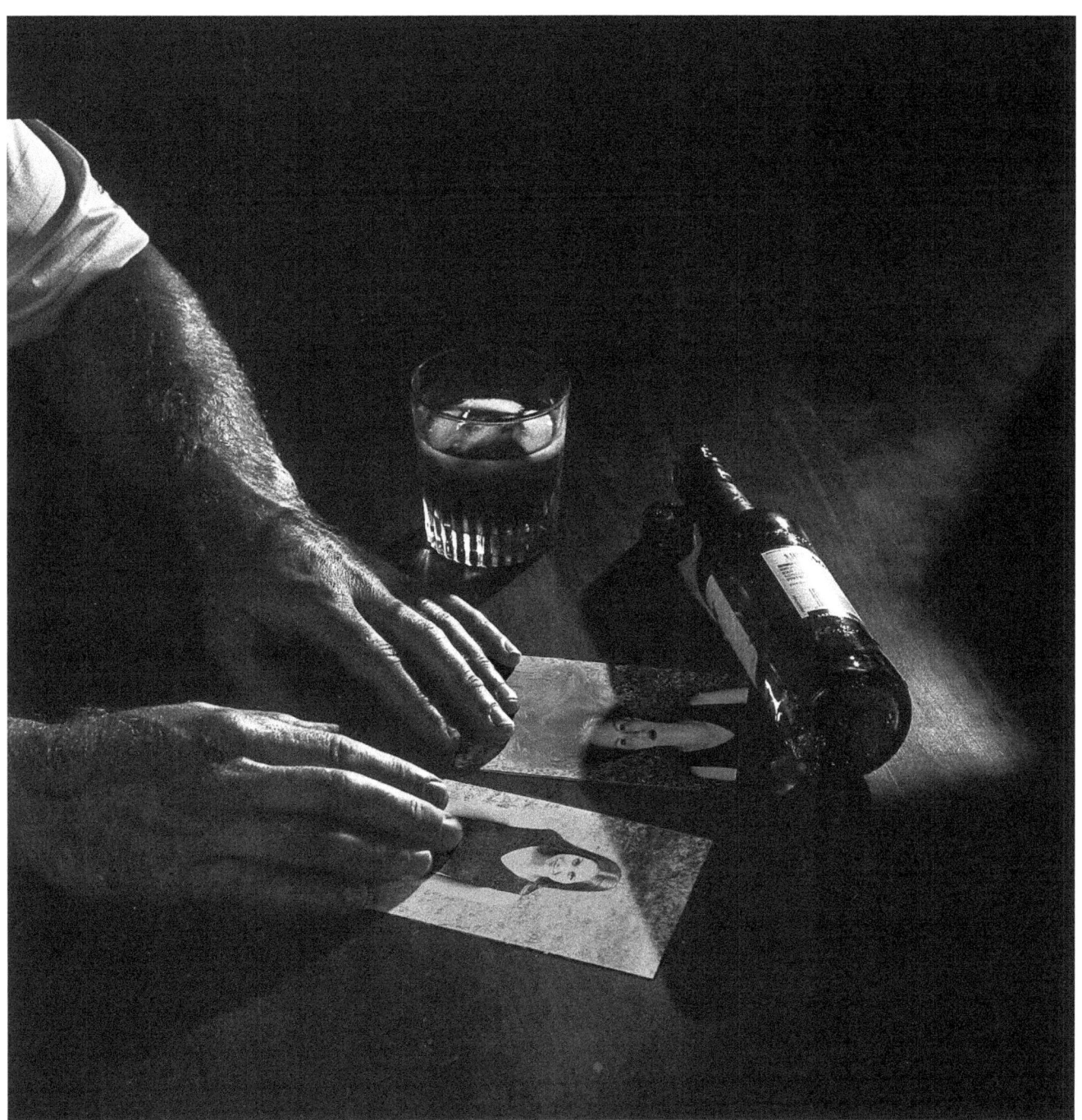

Lenity

Torment, heartache, wasted time,
and wasted all on you.
Nothing left of what we built
with nothing left to do

Trust in us and what that meant
means very little now.
This is not my fault, wish we
could press reset somehow

Can we go back, when we had
happy ever after?
With all we ever wanted,
life and love and laughter?

Nostalgic dreams, years ago
we never seemed to fight.
If I recall why and how
could we go back, tonight?

Even though it hurts me so,
this broken heart is tough.
For now, forgive, forget and
for us, that is enough

Reason

Why

Every action has an effect,
every effect, a cause.
There is a why for everything

But then... is why the same as cause?
Is there a reason
wherever there is a cause?

Does reason lose its validity
when emotions run hot or high?
When people are foolish or insane or stupid or in love?

Who cares

Go ahead,
get all caught up in it.
See where that gets you

Better to ask yourself, *does it matter?*
If the answer is *no*, then stop.
Sometimes, there is no why

Subtleties

A casual observation
about intent and perception...

If you had forgotten
to do something,
left something out
or incomplete,
or redundant,
or unexplainably *different*

I would expect you to fix it.
It would be evidence
of error

But in doing it slightly wrong,
purposefully,
for artistic reasons
or to send a
meaningful message,
you could be augmenting its worth
subtly, aesthetically

Understanding this,
I may very well value it

even to the point
that I may argue with you later
when you change your mind
and decide to do it right.
Because as off as it first appears,
it is better

The trick is to make it
Just obvious enough
But not too much so

It is preferable that most will find this
difficult to comprehend.
After all, it is in this,
the struggle to understand,
that there is as much
or often, even more value
than in the comprehension itself

That Thing That Was Missing

Something was missing,
I had not been feeling myself.
I was beholden to a slow, painless burn

What made it so frustrating,
I did not know what it was, that thing that was missing.
Could not put a finger on it

The whole ordeal was
incessant, incurable melancholy.
I kept searching, resolutely, always hunting

And at certain times I thought I found it,
that thing that was missing.
But it always turned out to be something else

Until now. And it was something I had not thought of before.
And as such, I had never truly looked for it.
And as it was, it came right to my front door and knocked

I opened the door and stood unmoving, staring, unbelieving.
Portentous, uncertain, intoxicating.
A leap of faith. It asked me if I wanted it, and of course, I said *yes*

Keeping in Mind

Holy crap, that guy is an idiot!
Dumber than a box of hammers!
Blurts ventromedial frontal lobe.
Nucleus accumbens grunts approval

Anterior insular cortex quickly intervenes.
Honestly, he is a nice guy and means well,
give him a break.
Nucleus accumbens again grunts approval

Parietal lobe chimes in.
It is true, he is a nice person, and it is a fact he is no Einstein,
though this is hardly worthy of a conversation.
Very small grunt

Ventral medial prefrontal cortex, who has been listening in all along, takes control.
Alright everyone, settle down.
Tell mouth to say nothing and to just smile, even if it does not want to.
After a prolonged moment, another grunt

The Nihility of Everything

I love to manipulate minds with proofs of string theory,
normalize novel ideas while quoting Madame Curie.
Ruminate the nuance of Nietzsche, the metaphysics of Foucault.
And for fun, influence a few financial market trends
with some obscure macroeconomic model

I find it simple to divine such things
as the relationship of rates of orbital decay
to the mutational tendencies of mitochondrial DNA.
Then, to gift the layman's version to my eyeless adherents
in pseudo-liturgical parlance, elaborated in elitist legalese with ease

Relentless, I amass terabytes of truth,
pausing periodically to polish and admire
my magnificent, monolithic mountain of erudition.
Within, a Niagara of knowledge to be launched at potential foes;
from a full mind, a roiling river of thought

Or to be aimed with precision and purpose,
a stream of consciousness, crafted carefully
to gain access, impress, influence and control.
To enlist and harness others
in the pursuit of prestige, property and power

Along the way, and on occasion some say
I should use it all to teach and team,
protect and improve, to harmonize and serve.
Foment and sustain symbiosis and responsibility.
To divine instead, relationships

That I should sympathize, empathize.
Pursue in lieu of a full mind, mindfulness.
They say that absent this, the value of all,
of everything, or nearly so
is nearly nothing

Want

The line between need and want,
whether fine or wide,
can be poorly interpreted
depending on the circumstances

What is
even more interesting
is the dilemma over
what is right

right now

versus what is right in the long run.
The immediately identifiable
ethical choice
measured against predictable, long-term effects

Morality versus reason,
personal code
shaped by religion and society
against outcomes-based decision making

Sage folk will tell me there is no conflict.
That the two should coincide.
That my heart and experience
will guide me

That there are friends and colleagues
and family I can confer with.
That if the decision is so difficult,
do not make it

right now

But a decision will need to be made eventually.
By that point, hopefully,
I will not still simply be trying to get
what I want

Still

There are a dozen reasons for me to react.
Instantly, without much thought.
A hundred coarse words lined up front to back on my tongue,
and forty-two facial muscles primed to contort and spasm

But I wait

A few of those muscles react unwittingly.
I realize when I notice my jaw hurts a bit.
Then I smile
at my marginally flawed attempt at composure

I wait and observe and something interesting happens,
a thing I did not expect.
Indeed, something close to what I had hoped for.
And though I had been forcing myself to relax all this time, I still let out a little

sigh of relief

Which makes me smile again.
And the smile stays as a dozen reasons vanish,
the words forgotten, spasmodic contortions averted,
and I move on thoughtfully to whatever life has lined up for me next

Look Inside

Evil is innate, I have found.
Ignored or misunderstood,
it develops insidiously
on its own

warping my ability to discern what is good or right.
The very thing I use to reason, the mind, is tainted
and at the same time, unaware of it.
How unfortunate, in a certain circular, intractable way…

However, this is reversible if I focus inward.
Once I understand, honestly embrace who I am,
what I am capable of, and what I most likely cannot do,
I have taken steps in the right direction

The evil is still there but is now recognized,
kept at bay by a genuine capacity to discriminate.
What follows is the world, clearly,
in all its beauty, complexity, and darkness

Sight

Clarity

With reckless abandon,
I blindly appraise the skies

Searching introspection
rewards me with open eyes

Grounded observation
separates the truth from lies

Musing

A veiled irony,
how true inspiration
so rarely comes from within.
Or if it does,
it is so personal,
it almost qualifies as selfishness

Someone else is usually involved.
Sometimes directly
and at other times,
in a seemingly inconsequential way

Yet, they are in most cases
somehow causal
in the revelatory,
the epiphany,
the pièce de résistance.
In the lightning strike

Move

Could be it is not all bad,
all crisis and regret.
Possible I have not had
the worst of worst days, yet

Perhaps I am standing still
while others move along.
It could be a test of will
that filters frail from strong

Will I ever start to move?
In this, I have a voice.
To myself, I need to prove
I can commit to choice

Weakness is to take a knee,
fear I will not succeed.
If I choose a destiny
and move, then I am freed

Spring

Tall crystal vases cast sunbeams astray,
sown round her figure, as if by design.
Reposed by the window, she smiles away
inquisitive, blessed, awaiting a sign

A luminous warmth caroms through the glass.
Indecisive, the resplendent bouquets
lured away, toward what might come to pass,
to the comfort of her lighthearted gaze

A radiant, blissful, questioning muse.
But what does she ask, and what does she know?
Lean to her, or the Sun? How can they choose
between an aurora and a rainbow?

She wonders what beauty may rise anew
and knows it starts within her, me and you

Au Courant

Thought of no one but myself for so long,
may have lost touch with society.
Imprisoned by so much critical thought,
I found I do not understand me

Looking inward, do my best to assess
what is in there that makes me unique.
Not afraid to be brutally honest
if what I find is markedly bleak

Acknowledging all my merits and flaws,
striving for empathy as the norm.
Armed with the thought I am not so pristine,
a translation of sorts starts to form

Rosetta for nearly everything else,
pushing unvarnished truth to the fore.
Clemency granted, the key in my mind,
au courant, I then walk through the door

The Lightness of Time

A million wild-colored florets
dancing rhythmically in the breeze

The sun spills warmth over the hills
as a doe darts through the tall grass

The child drops her fistful of blooms,
surprised, wide-eyed in sheer delight

Rarefied, the moment
now part of my soul

Life

Darkness falls, I am way behind,
I have too much to do.
To tend vexations in my mind,
some are old, others new

In dire need of ardent care,
suspect you need some too.
A little here, a little there,
take heart, my aim is true

Sun is rising, here comes the day.
Mind is clear, thanks to you.
All is good in every way,
one more time—*I want to*

Keep A Light On

Lurid and controversial thoughts often find cover
in a shaped and polished façade.
Tatemae born of honne, the negative filtered out.
What is left is often largely positive, genuine, or not

Yin and yang, fundamentally different yet symbiotic.
I will never see one but for the other,
as day has no meaning absent the dark
nor night without light, good without bad, right without wrong

This leads to a question.
In a perfect world, if everyone always did the right thing,
if bad were a foreign concept, would there be no good at all?
I could argue a world like this would be a terribly flawed place

As it is, humans are individually imperfect.
I make mistakes and try as best I can to learn from them.
As long as I continuously strive to improve
without replaying my misdeeds

I will remember where the dark used to be.
I remember what it looked like.
What it felt like, what it did to me, what it did to others,
and I will keep the light on

Serenity

Reminiscence

Slow falls the snow.
Laughing, glasses clinking

Cheery conversation, anticipation,
new beginnings

But I am entranced, by the window.
Lost in the silent ballet

of countless crystalline miracles
dancing gracefully down

to alight on white obscurity
and I find myself imploring the wind

Keep them aloft,
just a little longer

The Perfect Pair

One in front and one behind.
Crossing paths, off again.
To and fro, separated.
Will they join? Who knows when

Similar in many ways,
one is left, one is right.
Each is moving opposite
all the day, half the night

Then they finally come to rest,
their time apart is done.
The perfect pair, made that way,
now side by side as one

At First Sight

Silver starlight blankets the cool night.
Our eyes reflecting something, suspecting,
could it be this is love?

Warm feeling all over, head reeling,
the slightest touch exciting us so much.
It felt a lot like love

Now together, until forever.
That cool, starry night our eyes were right.
At first sight, it was love

Ne Plus Ultra

Cool, clear air.
Oxygen thick.
Inhale slowly,
measured, controlled.
Sunbeams peek between trees,
cutting the chill just enough.
Sharp report,
adrenaline rush,
and we go

Instant warmth.
Coursing, energized.
School of fish
bumping shoulders.
Field of view narrows.
The goal,
unseen but known,
one simple distance ahead

Find a nice pocket
and settle in.
Sounds muddle together,
overcome by rhythm.
Droplets of perspiration

tingling the brow.
Proof of purpose

Personal space
silently agreed upon.
Each of us
in our own little world.
Counting up, counting down
intermediate milestones

Endorphin kick,
riding the wave, euphoric endurance.
Good time
to break from tunnel vision

Glancing left and right,
quick smiles exchanged,
shared empathy acknowledged.
Only we know this.
Pace, breath, life,
synchronized

Carry the distance.
Passing some, passed by others

No matter, the goal is common
but the purpose is mine.
Banner ahead.
Cheering cuts through
a monotonous
drumroll of footfalls.
Break rhythm to embrace speed.
We shared the distance,
but suddenly it is more personal

Each remaining second
more important
than peaking pain.
Finish, exhilaration,
waves of emotion.
Vision goes wide,
colors and sounds
back in tune, bright and crisp

Pats on the back.
Grateful for these moments
Breathe it all in.
This is one way I know
life is beautiful

Rhapsody

Passion everywhere.
Anywhere, here.
And her, picture-perfect.
Impossibly beautiful,
leaning gracefully against the doorframe, smiling.
Only to turn and walk slowly away,
glancing back
to smile once more

A passion so real,
so intense,
so complete.
The kind of love
most never experience for even a
brief moment,
settling instead for a glimpse of its shadow
at the edge of their dreams

Perfect Day

Leaves dancing, rustling,
delicately caressed
by the soft breeze.
A whispered wind song

Patches of sun, darting,
break through branches,
cascade and collide in prismatic collage
on the forest floor

Nestled in shade,
mossed rocks, mushrooms
and unfurled ferns scattered
along my earthen path

I close my eyes and inhale gently.
Entranced, yet acutely aware of my role here,
an indelible, wonderful part of something
inestimably greater than myself

Celestial Reverie

Inspiration in elevation,
thoughts of having seen you so soon

A wingspread volante sensation
that propelled us over the moon

Vivid memory of tomorrow,
soaring paradiso by night

A skyward reflection foretelling
shooting stars, together in flight

This

The moment your sweet smile
elevated me, asked for nothing,
warmed my world-worn heart,
validated my existence

With an honest, nova-bright life in your eyes,
that purest expression of a want
only to love, only me.
I was overcome

A sublime, singular smile.
Ethereal, unconditional, real.
This, from then to now and ever on
is the memory by which I measure joy

Being Human

Knowing what needs to be done is the simple piece,
and that in itself can be formidable.
You will expend a lot of effort trying to figure that out.
You may think you are getting there
when you have identified what is wrong, what is right,
what you can fix by yourself, what you need help with,
and when to sit back and enjoy the entirety of it

You might write down the important parts and study it.
Discuss it with others,
assign value to their opinions,
go about reassessing, refining, *and and and*

Then to begin living it.
Some of it easy, much of it wonderful,
and on certain days it is incredibly difficult.
Your approach could be day by day
and you may concede that you will decide
to ignore your own plan at times.
Because you are admittedly flawed

Human after all

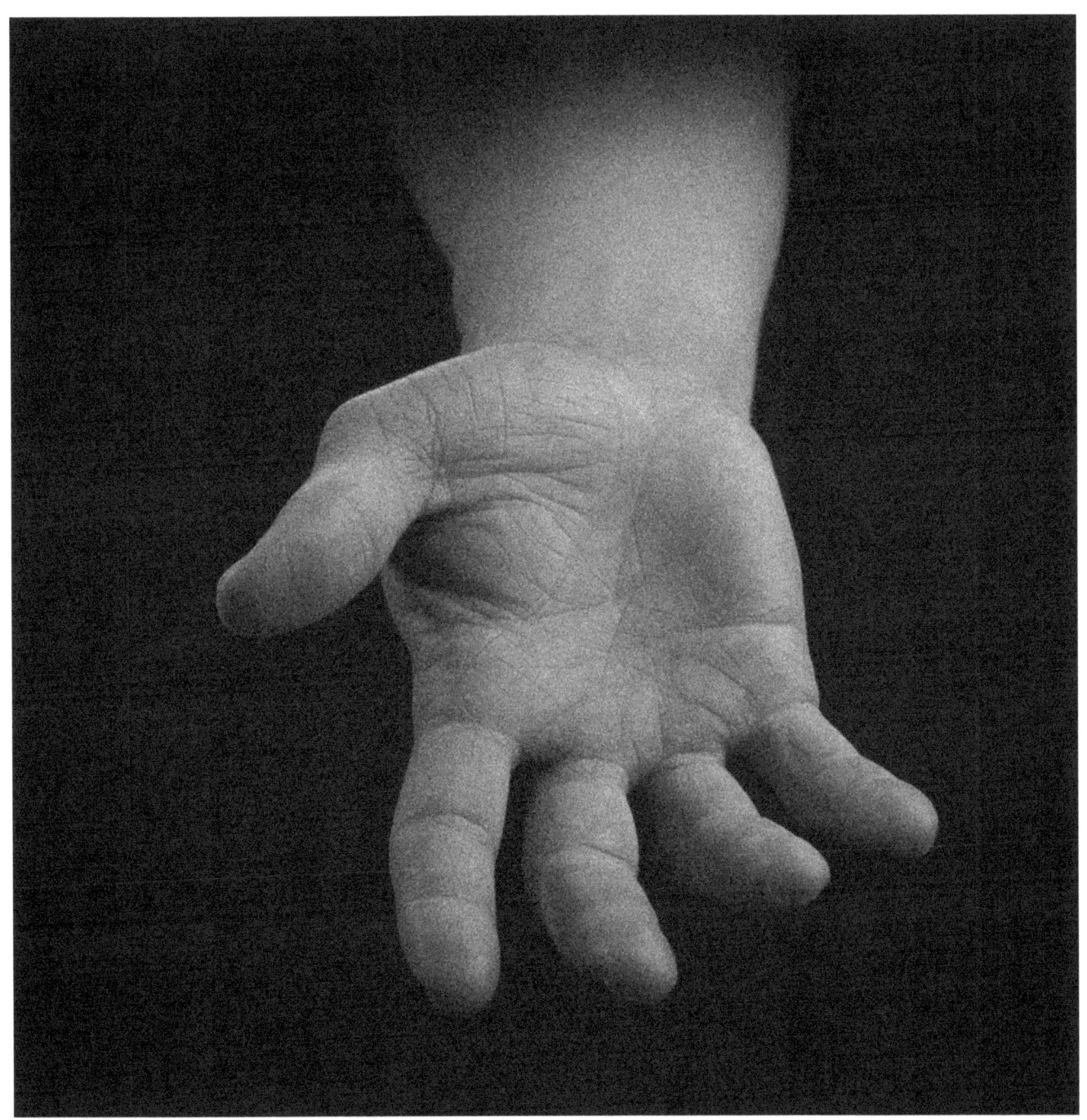

Φ

What is the meaning of life?

The verb 'to live' is often relegated to passive status, defined as 'a condition of existence'. When it is interpreted as an action verb it suggests living has *to be done, accomplished*. Watch a sunrise. Go for a run. Build something grand, have a family and share it all with them and others.

Complicating things…when we are preoccupied with *how things should have been done* or *what we wish we could do* we are left with a void of inaction in the present that without constraint, can quickly extrapolate into a reality that falls short of our abilities and expectations. We become both mentally and physically absent from life, emotionally lost in a past or future that have no value or bearing on the present—on our reality. As inattention to life carries on, this behavior can then lead to an unfortunate and circular dependency on the aforementioned preoccupation.

"The trouble is, you think you have time." Gautama Buddha expresses here that there are no such things as the future or past—they do not exist at all. It is the present now and at noon yesterday, it was the present then. When noon tomorrow arrives, it will also be the present. The present is all there is. *Now* is all we ever have for action, for living. Everything else is either historical or hypothetical, immutable data and uncertain potentialities that can be learned from and planned for—today. When I think in this manner, life begins to define itself. The meaning of life is *to live*.

Acknowledgements

Anna Apostolova: *her*

Roman Katok: *him*

Most of those who collaborated in the creation of *Raw Thoughts* joined me again for *Meridian*, and I am beyond grateful to have worked once more with such a talented and dedicated team. Anna and Roman reprised their roles as the human element for a majority of the photos. Victoria McIntosh returned as our exceptionally gifted hair and makeup artist for the multi-day shoot in Vermont. Amy Christiansen-Schoefman from *Eat More Cake* created and donated exceptionally decadent cupcakes for the *Want* photo. And of course, Scott Hussey's penchant for perfection and singularly artistic contribution is found on nearly every other page, in each photo, every raw thought. Thank you so much everyone for your help in making *Meridian* a beautiful reality.

As I mention in the foreword, this book is 'more refined' than the last. Just as the emotionally unvarnished nature of *Raw Thoughts* was intentional and important to the underlying philosophy of the book, so is something of the opposite true for *Meridian*. Teaming with Lauren Pilcher, a uniquely talented creative writing editor, was essential to perfect in *Meridian* what was purposefully left out of *Raw Thoughts* so it would stand on its own as a compelling and influential work of art and at the same time, succeed as a sequel. I am grateful to you, Lauren.

About the Author

JOHN CASEY is a Pushcart Prize-nominated poet and novelist from New Hampshire. He authored *Raw Thoughts: A mindful Fusion of Poetic and Photographic Art* in 2019, which was nominated for the National Book Award and Griffin Poetry Prize. He followed with *Meridian: A Raw Thoughts Book* in 2021. His poetry has been published internationally in numerous literary journals and magazines. Casey is the author of *Devolution* and *Evolution* as well, books one and two of The Devolution Trilogy. *Revelation* is the capstone to the psychological spy thriller series. A Veteran combat and test pilot with a Master of Arts from Florida State University, Casey also served as a diplomat and international affairs strategist at U.S. embassies in Germany and Ethiopia, the Pentagon, and elsewhere. He is passionate about fitness, nature, and the human spirit and inspired by the incredible spectrum of people, places, and cultures he has experienced in life.

www.ingramcontent.com/pod-product-compliance
Lightning Source LLC
Chambersburg PA
CBHW051257110526
44589CB00025B/2855